# Northern Elephant Seal Monitoring (*Mirounga angustirostris*) at Point Reyes National Seashore

*2008–2009 Breeding Seasons*

Natural Resource Technical Report NPS/SFAN/NRTR—2012/649

Sarah Allen, Sarah Codde[1], Heather Jensen, Elizabeth Wheeler[2], Ben Becker, Dave Press, and Dale Roberts[1]

Point Reyes National Seashore
1 Bear Valley Road
Point Reyes Station, CA 94956

[1]San Francisco Bay Area Inventory and Monitoring Program
Point Reyes National Seashore
1 Bear Valley Road
Point Reyes Station, CA 94956

[2]The Marine Mammal Center
Fort Cronkite
2000 Bunker Road
Sausalito, California 94965

July 2012

U.S. Department of the Interior
National Park Service
Natural Resource Stewardship and Science
Fort Collins, Colorado

The National Park Service, Natural Resource Stewardship and Science office in Fort Collins, Colorado publishes a range of reports that address natural resource topics of interest and applicability to a broad audience in the National Park Service and others in natural resource management, including scientists, conservation and environmental constituencies, and the public.

The Natural Resource Technical Report Series is used to disseminate results of scientific studies in the physical, biological, and social sciences for both the advancement of science and the achievement of the National Park Service mission. The series provides contributors with a forum for displaying comprehensive data that are often deleted from journals because of page limitations.

All manuscripts in the series receive the appropriate level of peer review to ensure that the information is scientifically credible, technically accurate, appropriately written for the intended audience, and designed and published in a professional manner.

This report received peer review by individuals who were not directly involved in the collection, analysis, or reporting of the data, and whose background and expertise put them on par technically and scientifically with the authors of the information. Data in this report were collected and analyzed using methods based on established, peer-reviewed protocols and were analyzed and interpreted within the guidelines of the protocols.

Views, statements, findings, conclusions, recommendations, and data in this report do not necessarily reflect views and policies of the National Park Service, U.S. Department of the Interior. Mention of trade names or commercial products does not constitute endorsement or recommendation for use by the U.S. Government.

This report is available from the San Francisco Bay Area Network Inventory and Monitoring website (http://science.nature.nps.gov/im/units/sfan) and the Natural Resource Publications Management website (http://www.nature.nps.gov/publications/nrpm/).

Please cite this publication as:

NPS 612/118228, December 2012

# Contents

# Contents (continued)

# Figures

# Tables

# Executive Summary

Northern elephant seals (*Mirounga angustirostris*) established a breeding population at Point Reyes National Seashore (PORE) in 1981 and since then the colony has grown steadily (Allen et al. 1989). Currently, elephant seals breed at numerous sites within PORE, with four primary sites located at Drake's Beach (DB), Point Reyes Headland (PRH), South Beach (SB), and Chimney Rock Loop (CRL). PORE began to monitor the elephant seal population to contribute to the understanding of population changes and management needs, and to develop research, interpretation and enforcement strategies. A pinniped monitoring protocol was developed in 2009 and includes objectives for monitoring elephant seals to determine trends population growth and productivity.

During December to March of each breeding season, we conducted a complete census a minimum of once per week at all four breeding sites. In 2008, 34 censuses were conducted, and in 2009, 28 surveys were conducted. Each season, flipper tags were applied to weaned pups, and weekly surveys were conducted to resight tagged animals. Reproductive productivity index was estimated as the number of pups compared to number of adult females.

Using a correction factor, we estimated a total breeding population size 1,845 and 1,988 seals at PORE in 2008 and 2009, respectively. Almost 20% more females were counted at DB colony sites in 2008 (247) compared with 2009 (198). Nearly twice as much rain was measured in the winter of 2008-2009 at Point Reyes compared to 2007-2008, but January 2008 monthly precipitation was greater than in January 2009. January is a time when pregnant females and newborn pups are more vulnerable. DB continued to be a more attractive colony site than PRH during winters with hazardous coastal weather and tide conditions coinciding with the initial arrival of females. In contrast, during the 2008-2009 winter when large storms did not occur until February, fewer females were displaced to DB from PRH. Instead, the number of females at PRH increased in 2009. SB female breeding population remained fairly constant between the two breeding seasons.

During the 2008-09 seasons, a total of 499 weaned elephant seal pups were tagged. In 2008, 51 adult seals were resighted (84 tag observations) with tags originally applied at PORE in previous years. In 2009, 57 adult seals were resighted (90 tag observations) as PORE seals. A total of 33 adult elephant seals tagged at other colonies were documented at PORE breeding sites during 2008 and 33 were observed in 2009.

The overall population productivity index was 0.77 in 2008 and 0.84 in 2009. Since 2005, there has been a slightly greater increase in productivity at the more recently colonized sites (DB, SB) compared with the remote and cliff-backed PRH site. Reduction of human disturbance through park-implemented signage, increased law enforcement near colonies, a docent program and greater public awareness have all contributed to the successful establishment of these peripheral sites. Some 60-70 wildlife docents logged over 4,000 hours for the two years combined, contacting a total of 18,000 to 19,000 people per year.

# Acknowledgments

The Marin Conservation Corps AmeriCorps Program members were key partners in the field and data management. The Marine Mammal Center also was an important partner in marine education and research. Many volunteers contributed to the elephant seal monitoring, including J. Bourke, J. Hall, W. Holter, J. Longstreth, E. Sojourner, E. Brody, S. Van Der Wal, and S. Waber. We are also grateful for collaborative discussions and exchange of information with D. Lee and R. Bradley of PRBO Conservation Science, P. Morris of the University of California Año Nuevo Natural Reserve, and B. Hatfield of US Geological Survey. This study was conducted under the National Marine Fisheries Service Permit 373-1868-00. We also thank R. Zeno for her contribution to data quality and analysis of elephant seal tag resight data from PORE with assistance from R. Condit and B. Becker. We are grateful to M. Lowry of NOAA Southwest Fisheries Center and P. Kleeman of the Biological Resources Division of the US Geological Survey for reviewing this report. We also thank R. Sauvajot, the Peer Review Manager for the Pacific West Region of the National Park Service.

The elephant seal monitoring program received financial support from Point Reyes National Seashore, the David and Vicki Cox Family Foundation, and the Point Reyes National Seashore Association. Thanks also to the Point Reyes National Seashore Elephant Seal Docent Program volunteers who spent many wintry hours to enthusiastically share the wonders of northern elephant seals to PORE visitors, guided and assisted by B. Lindquist and M. Repko.

# Introduction

Northern elephant seals (*Mirounga angustirostris*) have re-established breeding colonies along the California coast since the 1950's (Stewart et al. 1994) and in 1981, the first northern elephant seal birth was recorded at an isolated pocket beach at the Point Reyes National Seashore (PORE; Allen et al. 1989). The colony has grown steadily since then with immigrants from other breeding colonies at the Channel Islands, Año Nuevo, Big Sur coast and the Southeast Farallon Islands, and more recently from San Simeon (Allen et al. 1989, Adams 1993, Sydeman and Allen 1999). The colony continued to grow exponentially until 1997, when an estimated 300 pups were produced (Sydeman and Allen 1999). Since 1997, the population growth rate slowed, but breeding elephant seals continued to expand into new sub-colonies within PORE.

Currently, northern elephant seals breed on beaches at numerous sites around Point Reyes Headland, but four sub-colonies are dominant; Point Reyes Headlands (PRH), Drake's Beach (DB; formerly called North Drakes Beach) , Chimney Rock Loop (CRL), and South Beach (SB). In response to the increase of the breeding population of seals within the park and associated park activities, the park created a Northern Elephant Seal Management Plan (Allen 1995) to (1) set guidelines for research, interpretation, and enforcement; (2) contribute to the understanding of population changes and possible further growth and management needs; and (3) to develop research, interpretation and enforcement strategies.

To fulfill these goals, PORE has been monitoring the elephant seal population size and productivity during the breeding season annually since 1995. For the period 2007-2009, the elephant seal population at PORE was monitored based on a pinniped protocol developed for the San Francisco Bay Area Inventory and Monitoring Program (SFAN; Adams et al. 2009). The objectives of the protocol are to determine long-term trends in annual population size, reproductive success, and annual and seasonal distribution at PORE and to identify potential or existing threats (Adams et al. 2009). The methods are outlined in this report to provide context to the reader. The 2005-2007 breeding seasons were summarized in Adams et al. 2008.

This report is a summary of the elephant seal breeding season monitoring program activities and results of the 2008-09 seasons. Because the northern elephant seal breeding season splits the calendar year, in this report the latter year is used to refer to the breeding season (i.e., December 2007 to March 2008 would be referred to as the 2008 season).

# Methods

## Study Site

Northern elephant seals breed at four main sub-colonies in the park: Point Reyes Headlands (PRH, a.k.a. main colony), the western extension of Drake's Beach (DB), Chimney Rock Loop (CRL; a.k.a. the eastern extension of Point Reyes Headland), and South Beach (SB, a.k.a. Southernmost section of Point Reyes Beach; Figure 1). These main breeding sites are divided into subsites, for more accurate counting. There are seven subsites at Point Reyes Headlands sub-colony: Cove 1 (C1), Cove 2 (C2), Cove 3 (C3), Cove 4 (C4), Tip Beach (TIP), Loser Beach (LB), and Dead Seal Beach (DSB). At South Beach sub-colony, there are three subsites: Lighthouse Beach (LTH), Nunes Ranch Beach (NUN), and Mendoza Ranch Beach (MEN). DB sub-colony has three subsites: Drakes Beach (DB), Drakes Nunes Beach (NUNB) and Drakes Mendoza Beach (MENB). Drakes Beach previously included the subsites Lifeboat Station (LBS), Gus's Cove (GUS), and Chimney Rock Cove (CRC) which are now combined separately into the Chimney Rock Loop (CRL) subsite (Figure 1).

In addition to the breeding sites, park staff and visitors reported elephant seals hauled out on several other beaches in the park (Limantour, Drakes Beach at the Ken Patrick Visitor Center, Kehoe Beach, and Double Point). We compiled these incidental reports, but these data are excluded from the breeding census counts, because they are not systematically surveyed. It is assumed that the breeding site censuses account for the animals (typically sub-adult males and immatures) that move among sites during the breeding season.

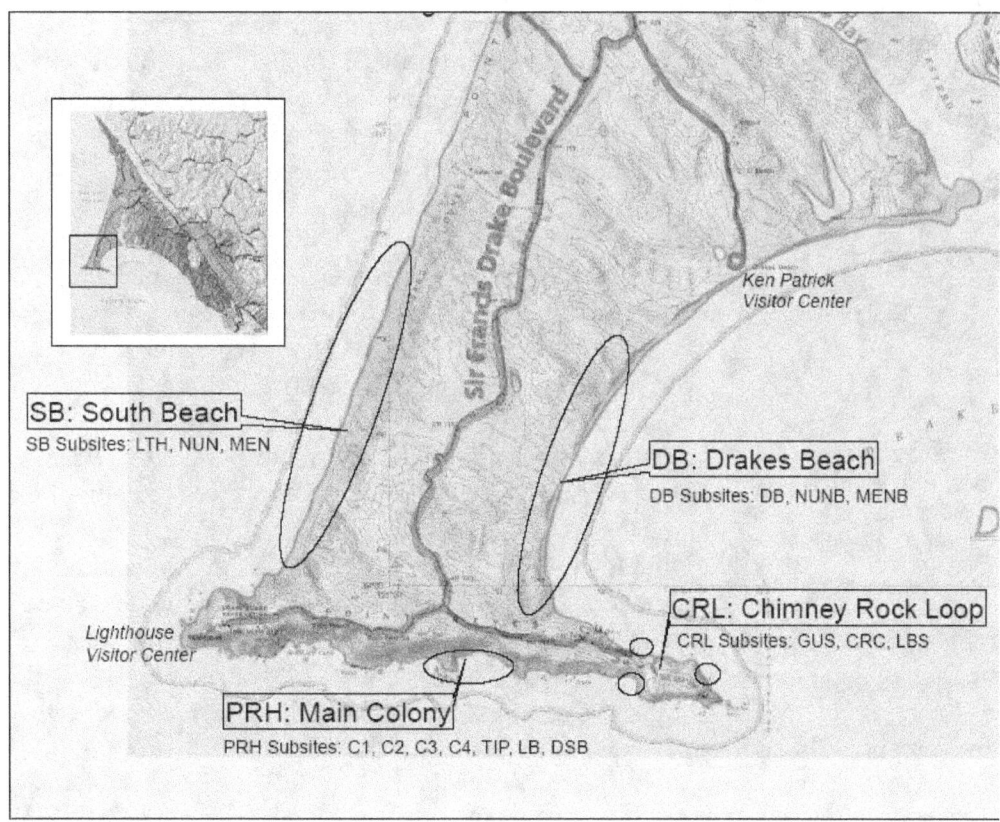

**Figure 1.** Northern elephant seal breeding sites at Point Reyes National Seashore.

## Field Methods

### Population and Productivity Surveys

From December 1 through March 15 of each breeding season, we conducted a complete census of elephant seals at least once per week at all breeding sites within the park (PRH, DB, CRL and SB), weather permitting (Figure 2). During the peak period of pupping from January to the end of February, we conducted two censuses per week to try to capture the peak adult female and pup/weaned pup counts (for age class descriptions see Adams et al. 2009). We counted seals from fixed vantage points on cliffs with the aid of a 40X spotting scope and 8-10X binoculars. We tallied sex and age groups within each sub-colony; adult female (Cow), bull male (Bull), sub-adult male classes 1-4 (SA1-4), immature (IMM), yearling (YRLNG), nursing pup (Pup; including dead pups), and weaned pup (WNR). Male age classes are determined by the extent of the chest shield, the length of the proboscis, and overall body length (LeBoeuf and Laws 1994). New observers were trained in the field by experienced observers to identify male age classes.

**Figure 2**. Marin Conservation Corps-Americorps member, Erin Flynn, surveying seals at Point Reyes Headland. Photograph by Heather Jensen.

### Survivorship and Site Fidelity

Individually marking animals allow researchers to estimate survivorship, site fidelity, and migration rates. Colony-specific tag color and serial numbers allow researchers to track individuals over many years, with the potential to also study individual animal productivity, and to identify the dispersal of seals from Point Reyes to other locations. Similar to the procedures at other northern elephant seal colonies, we applied individually numbered plastic tags (Dalton brand) to the hind flipper of weaned pups born at PORE under National Marine Fisheries Service (NMFS) permit 373-1868-00.

Until 1998, the number of weaned pups tagged each year roughly approximated the total number of pups surviving to weaning; however, currently the goal as outlined in the Pinniped Monitoring Protocol (Adams et al. 2009) is to tag 200-300 weaned pups each year as representative of the population born in a given year. Here we simply report the number of weaned pups single or double tagged in the cohort of each year. Double-tagging (tagging both hind flippers) is often done to estimate tag loss and to increase the chance of resighting an animal, since both flippers are not always visible. At PORE, double-tagging has been done opportunistically and the sample size of double tags is currently insufficient to estimate tag loss. When possible, we also tag and dye-mark a few adult males to track inter-site and inter-colony movement within a season.

Surveys to resight tagged individuals occurred weekly on the easily accessible beaches (DB, SB, GUS); while resight surveys at PRH sites occurred only in December, early January and March because of concerns for human safety. The PRH sites have difficult access and a higher density of seals. We recorded tag information from animals during resight surveys. Information recorded during resight surveys included: location of seal, flipper tag number, color, side (left or right), and position among the inter-digit webs (round or square). We also recorded the presence or absence of tags on the other flipper. Animals with freeze brand marks (applied at other breeding colonies) and distinctive scars such as shark bites were recorded as notes. If the animal was an adult-sized female, we recorded whether she was with a nursing pup, and the pup size class (P1-4). If the animal was a sub-adult 4 or bull male, we recorded whether it was dominant on the beach (Alpha), sub-dominant (Beta), or not associated with females (NA).

Temporary dye-marking was used in some years to identify individual breeding adults, and to document adult and sub-adult male movement. Dye marks allow individual identification without needing to read the tags each visit during a season. We applied dye-marks with human hair dye (Lady Clairol, Natural Blue-Black) using the applicator bottle. We used a series of individual alpha-numeric codes to dye-mark animals, using the first letter to denote the first site the animal was observed (i.e., "D2" is the second seal marked at the DB site). If possible, marks were placed on the back and side of the animal to insure good visibility of the mark from a distance. The orientation and shape of the dye-mark was recorded on a "scar card" to help field staff identify difficult to read dye marks during subsequent observations. The hair dye is innocuous to the seals and the mark disappears after the annual molt. In addition, marked males have increased the ability of volunteer docents to track individuals from the Elephant Seal Overlook above the DB site and educate park visitors about the monitoring study.

## Analytical Methods

### Data Management
All data gathered during the breeding season was entered into a Microsoft Access XP database maintained at PORE. The survey data was entered on a weekly basis and the resight and tagging data was entered on a bi-monthly basis. Error checking procedures within the database were used and all data entered were checked against the raw data sheets at the end of the season (see Adams et al. 2009). Since the previous report of 2005-2007 (Adams et al. 2008) the database on tagged animals has been thoroughly updated, and some data reported in that document may vary slightly from this report.

### Population Size
Breeding population estimates were based on maximum survey counts for sex and age groups by colony (Allen et al. 1989). An accurate total population size was not possible during the breeding season since not all age classes are present on the beaches. NMFS estimates the elephant seal population size by using raw pup counts multiplied by the inverse of expected ratio of pups to total animals based on a paper by McCann (1985). Barlow et al. (1993) recommended using 3.5 as an appropriate multiplier for a rapidly growing population such as the California stock of northern elephant seals. The PORE population estimates were based on the pup count multiplier (3.5) used with the maximum total of the combined weaned pup and pup (live and dead) count by colony or subsite. Condit et al. (2007) proposed another estimator for total population size based on a Bayesian analytical approach, and after review of the pinniped monitoring protocol, our future analyses of PORE females may include this estimator.

## Productivity

We used a standardized productivity index similar to the Southeast Farallon Island study (Lee 2006). The index was determined by using the following formula:

$$\frac{\text{Maximum count of pups*}}{\text{Estimated total number of adult females**}} = \text{Productivity Index}$$

* Maximum count of pups is the sum of the weaned pups, nursing pups and dead pups at time x.
** Estimate of total number of adult females present at rookery during breeding season includes the number of females counted 33 days prior and after the maximum count.

The productivity index was calculated for colony sites and the population. We estimated the total number of breeding females using the weekly mean - maximum count of adult females during peak pupping (approximately 27 January to 3 February) adjusted by including the adult female counts 33 days prior and 33 days after the peak count for each colony site (Adams 1993; LeBoeuf and Laws 1994; Table 1).

#adult females at peak + #adult females 33 days prior to peak + #adult females 33 days after peak = Estimate of total number of adult females

This adjustment takes into account females that depart early and those that have not yet arrived at the time of the peak count (average female stay at colony is 6 days prior to pupping + 27 days nursing period; LeBoeuf and Laws 1994), but does not take into account the adult female natality rate (the proportion of adult females actually birthing in a given year; see Adams et al. 2009). This method to determine productivity assumes that we are able to capture the high count of pups plus weaners and adult females during the bi-weekly surveys and that female natality is unknown but relatively stable across years. The index reflects productivity only and not mortality (dead pups are included in the total) that occurred at the breeding site. We calculated pup mortality based on the number of weaned pups present at the end of the breeding season divided by the estimated total number of females present (see definition above). Condit et al. (2007) proposed another estimator for total female count per year, and after review of the pinniped monitoring protocol, our future analyses of PORE females may include this estimator.

## Survivorship and Site Fidelity

Currently, we are participating in a range-wide tag resight analysis with managers and university researchers working at other elephant seal monitoring sites, the results of which are preliminary (Zeno et al. 2010).

# Results

## Population surveys

We conducted censuses each breeding season at primary colony sites (PRH, DB, SB, CRL) and at smaller sites from December through March. In 2007-08, 34 censuses (24 complete and 10 partial surveys) were conducted; in 2008-09, 28 (17 complete and 11 partial surveys) were conducted. Counts during tag-resight surveys were not included in these results. Population size and productivity data for 2006-07 are provided for comparison. Breeding population estimates and productivity index values in Table 1 are weighted means calculated from total figures and not simple means of the value for each of the colony site or subsite.

**Table 1.** Point Reyes National Seashore northern elephant seal counts and estimates for 2007 - 2009 breeding seasons at each colony site. The 2007 breeding season is included for comparisons among years.

| Season | Colony site[1] | Max count of adult females | Estimated total number of adult females[2] | Total number of births[3] | Breeding population size estimate[4] | Overall population estimate[5] | Productivity index[5&6] |
|---|---|---|---|---|---|---|---|
| 2007 | PRH | 362 | 387 | 374 | 722 | 1309.0 | 0.97 |
| | SB | 24 | 25 | 24 | 75 | 84.0 | 0.96 |
| | DB | 145 | 154 | 147 | 294 | 514.5 | 0.95 |
| | CRL | 127 | 130 | 105 | 210 | 367.5 | 0.81 |
| | Total | 658 | 705 | 650 | 1301 | 2275.0 | 0.92 |
| 2008 | PRH | 292 | 313 | 225 | 565 | 787.5 | 0.72 |
| | SB | 25 | 25 | 24 | 76 | 84.0 | 0.96 |
| | DB | 230 | 247 | 212 | 366 | 742.0 | 0.86 |
| | CRL | 93 | 98 | 66 | 159 | 231.0 | 0.67 |
| | Total | 648 | 683 | 527 | 1166 | 1844.5 | 0.77 |
| 2009 | PRH | 317 | 348 | 283 | 649 | 990.5 | 0.81 |
| | SB | 16 | 19 | 19 | 57 | 66.5 | 1.00 |
| | DB | 172 | 198 | 152 | 324 | 532.0 | 0.77 |
| | CRL | 117 | 125 | 113 | 245 | 395.5 | 0.90 |
| | Total | 622 | 680 | 568 | 1275 | 1988.0 | 0.84 |

[1] Peak census of adult females includes all sub-colonies

[2] Estimate of the total number of adult females during the breeding season includes the number of females counted 33 days prior and after the peak count.

[3] The maximum count of live and dead pups plus weaned pups on a single census for each colony site.

[4] The maximum survey count of all seals including pups.

[5] Based on pup count correction factor of 3.5 (see methods section).

[6] Maximum number of young divided by the adjusted maximum number of adult females.

**Productivity**

As in past years, the peak number of adult females (cows) at the rookery during the breeding season occurred during the last week of January and first week of February (Figures 3, 4, and 5; Adams et al. 2008). In 2008, the peak number of adult females counted for all sites was on 1/30/2008; adult female peak counts at sub-colonies occurred at SB and DB on 1/30/2008, and PRH on 2/1/2008. In 2009, the peak number of females for all sites was on 1/28/2009; sub-colony female peak counts occurred at PRH on 1/28/09 and at SB and DB on 1/30/09. The first pups were recorded during the 2007-08 (i.e., 2008 breeding season) breeding season on 12/19/07 at PRH, 12/24/07 at DB and 1/07/08 at SB; and during the 2008-09 (i.e., 2009 breeding season) season on 12/23/08 at PRH, 12/31/08 at DB and 1/6/09 at SB. The peak number of pups, dead pups and weaned pups (combined counts) was 527 on 02/15/08 and 568 on 02/3/09. The first pup born at PRH in 2008 was born at the DSB sub-colony where a large landslide during the previous winter had deposited an enormous amount of sand that had enlarged the sandy beach where seals haul out.

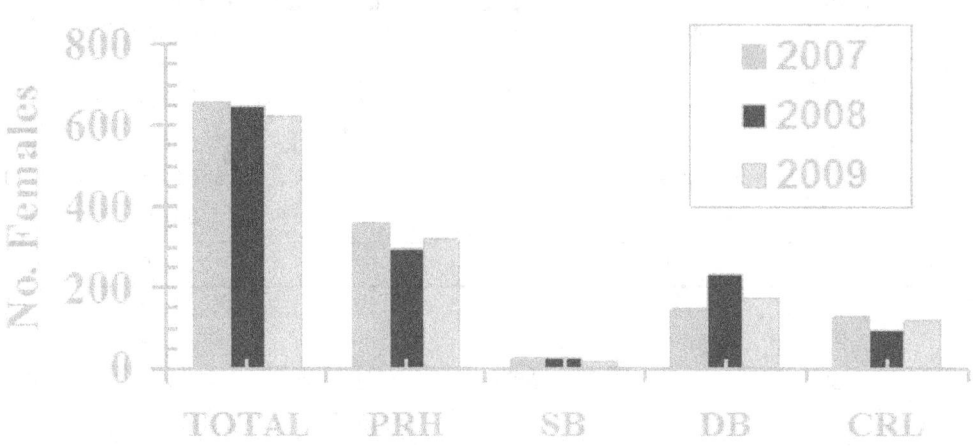

**Figure 3.** The maximum number of adult females at Point Reyes and at each sub-colony by year.

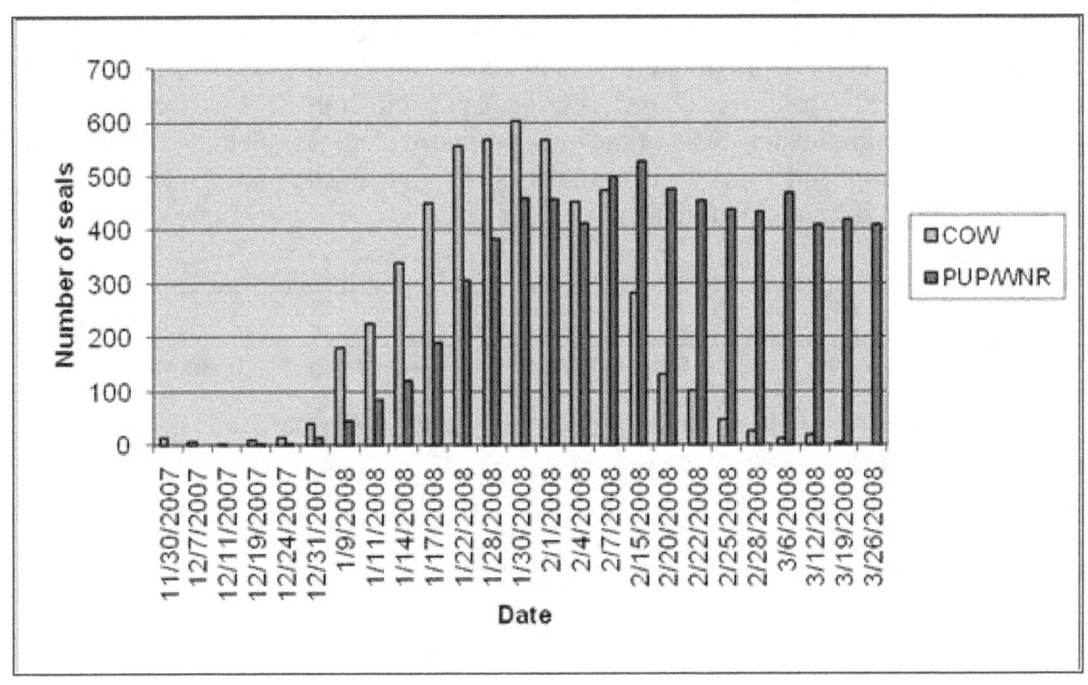

**Figure 4.** Number of northern elephant seal cows, and pup and weaned pups combined at Point Reyes National Seashore during the 2008 breeding season by survey date.

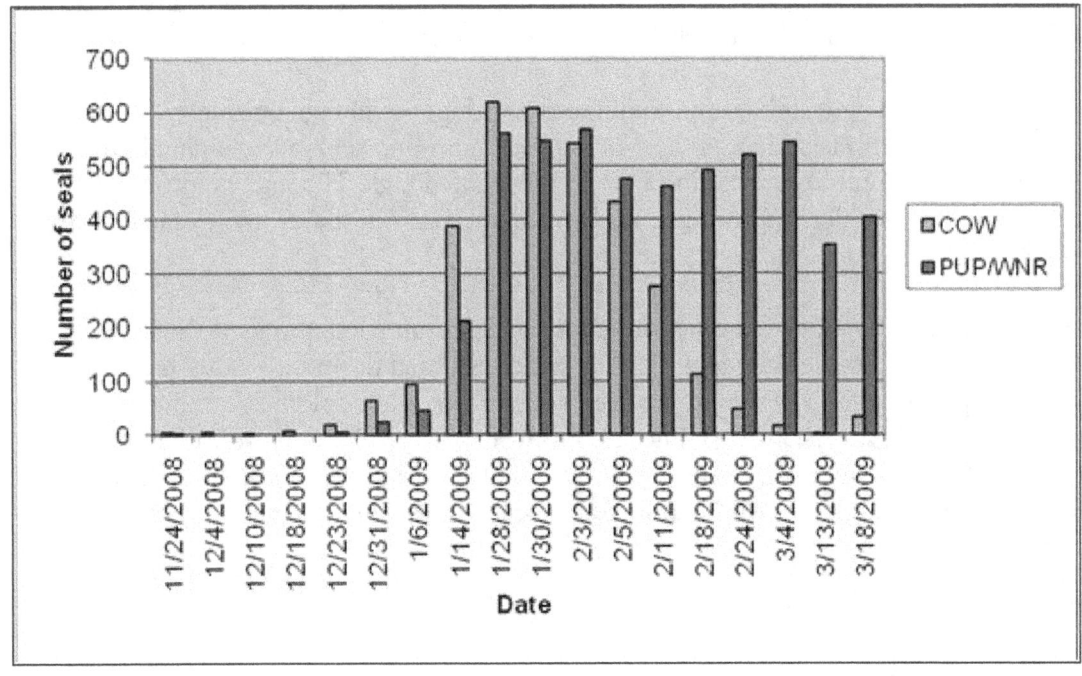

**Figure 5.** Number of northern elephant seal cows, and pup and weaned pups combined at Point Reyes National Seashore during the 2009 breeding season by survey date.

## Survivorship and Site Fidelity

The number of pups to survive to weaning in 2008 was 463 and in 2009 was 543, yielding a mortality estimate to weaning of approximately 32% in 2008 and 20% in 2009. During the 2008 pupping season, a total of 226 seals were tagged as weaned pups; in 2009, 273 weaned pups were tagged (Table 2). Approximately 50% of the pups produced were tagged both in 2008 and 2009. In 2008, biologists applied temporary dye-marks to 11 (adult and sub-adult males) seals and in 2009, 4 seals (adult and sub-adult males).

**Table 2.** Number of northern elephant seals flipper tagged at Point Reyes National Seashore by year, age class and sex.

| Breeding season | | Adult | | Sub-adult Male | | Weaned pup | | Unknown | Total |
|---|---|---|---|---|---|---|---|---|---|
| | | Female | Bull | SA4 | SA3 | Male | Female | | |
| 2008 | Seals tagged | 0 | 2 | 2 | 0 | 83 | 53 | 90 | 230 |
| | Single | 0 | 2 | 2 | 0 | 77 | 49 | 89 | 219 |
| | Double | 0 | 0 | 0 | 0 | 6 | 4 | 1 | 11 |
| 2009 | Seals tagged | 0 | 1 | 0 | 0 | 103 | 79 | 91 | 274 |
| | Single | 0 | 1 | 0 | 0 | 95 | 74 | 87 | 257 |
| | Double | 0 | 0 | 0 | 0 | 8 | 5 | 4 | 17 |

## Tag Resighting

The amount of effort expended to resight tags varied among years. The frequency of resight surveys depended on a number of factors including access to sites, size of colony and access to particular animals (i.e., it is easier to read tags of males and yearlings because they are located on the fringe of the colony compared to females), and ratio of animals on the beach.

In 2008, 51 non-pup seals were sighted (84 total tag resightings) with tags originally applied at PORE, representing 0.61 of the resighted tags. In 2009, 57 non-pup seals were sighted (90 total tag resightings) as PORE seals, representing 0.63 of the sighted tags. The highest proportion of seals sighted were adult females, followed by multiple age classes of males, then yearlings and weaned pups.

A total of 35 seals originally tagged at other colonies were documented at one of the PORE breeding sites during the 2008 season; and 33 seals were resighted during the 2009 breeding season (Table 3; Appendix A). The majority of seals seen from other colonies came from Año Nuevo (green tag) and Piedras Blancas (white) tags, but seals were also seen from San Nicolas Island (red), San Miguel/Santa Rosa Islands (yellow), Punta Gorda (purple), Benitos Islands, Baja California (blue), and releases of rehabilitated animals from The Marine Mammal Center (orange).

**Table 3.** Number of flipper tagged northern elephant seals sighted at Point Reyes National Seashore by year, age class and sex, and by colony. Proportion is the proportion of tagged seals sighted from other colonies for the year.

| Year | Colony | Age | | Sex | | Total Count | Proportion |
|------|--------|-----|-----|-----|-----|-----|-----|
| **2007-08** | | Adult | Immature | Female | Male | | |
| | Año Nuevo | 6 | 3 | 6 | | 9 | 0.11 |
| | Farallones | 0 | | | | 0 | 0.00 |
| | Piedras Blancas | 15 | 1 | 10 | 4 | 15 | 0.18 |
| | Punta Gorda | 1 | | 1 | | 1 | 0.01 |
| | San Nicolas | 3 | | 3 | | 2 | 0.02 |
| | San Miguel | 3 | | 3 | | 3 | 0.04 |
| | San Benitos | | 1 | 1 | | 1 | 0.01 |
| | TMMC | 2 | | 1 | 1 | 2 | 0.02 |
| | Point Reyes | 46 | 5 | 30 | 16 | 51 | 0.61 |
| | Total | | | | | 84 | 1.00 |
| **2008-09** | | | | | | | |
| | Año Nuevo | 4 | 6 | 2 | 2 | 10 | 0.11 |
| | Farallones | 1 | | 1 | | 1 | 0.01 |
| | Piedras Blancas | 10 | 6 | 6 | 3 | 15 | 0.17 |
| | Punta Gorda | 1 | | 1 | | 1 | 0.01 |
| | San Nicolas | | | | | 0 | 0.00 |
| | San Miguel | 3 | 1 | 3 | | 4 | 0.04 |
| | San Benitos | | | | | 0 | 0.00 |
| | TMMC | 2 | | 1 | 1 | 2 | 0.02 |
| | Point Reyes | 48 | 8 | 37 | 11 | 57 | 0.63 |
| | Total | | | | | 90 | 1.00 |

# Discussion

## Population Size and Productivity

The timing of the peak annual population size at each sub-colony during the breeding season was similar to previous survey years, occurring at PRH sub-colonies in 2007-8 on January 30 and February 1, and in 2008-09 on January 28 and 30. The timing of the first birth for both seasons also was similar to previous years, occurring in mid to late December. As DB sub-colony has matured, the date of first birth has occurred earlier compared to when the nascent sub-colony was composed of young females in 1995. Although SB sub-colony formed the same year as DB in 1995, it has not grown and the date of first birth remains later in the season; the first births occurred during the first week of January in both 2008 and 2009. The peak number of pups and weaned pups combined for all sub-colonies varied between late January (2008) and early February (2009), and is likely related to both the timing of most births and storm events that move weaned pups around. Combining all age and sex classes, the peak count was 1,210 elephant seals on 1/30/08 and 1,320 on 1/28/09.

The overall population estimate in 2008 declined by 19% compared to 2007 and in 2009 remained 13% lower than 2007. Reshuffling of animals likely occurred between sub-colonies. For example, the overall population estimate at PRH declined by 40% (1309 and 787) between 2007 and 2008, but at DB increased by 44 % (514 and 742). Extreme waves generated by storms in winter that coincide with the arrival of pregnant females likely influence where females eventually settle to give birth, and often DB is more appealing to females because of the lower wave action compared to PRH and SB (Pettee 1999; see below). The productivity for all sites combined was lower in 2008 compared to 2007 by nearly 20% which was most apparent in the decline of females at PRH (Table 1). Overall productivity in 2009 again remained lower than 2007 by 9% but was higher than 2008. Again, seals at PRH accounted for much of the decline.

The Chimney Rock Cove (CRC), a growing subsite of the Chimney Rock Loop (CRL), continued to have large numbers of adult females in 2008 and 2009, (n=53 and n=60, respectively), but not as many as the maximum number observed in 2007 (n=87 females). Gus's Cove, also part of the CRL, had lower numbers of adult females and weaned pups in 2008 which was reflected in lower productivity (0.67; see Table 1) but recovered in 2009 (0.90). CRC and Gus's Cove of CRL have a southern exposure at the headlands and receive more wave action than most other subsites. In recent years, researchers have noticed an increase in sand deposition at the pocket beaches, which could account for the higher numbers. At PRH, the DSB subsite continued to accommodate numerous adult females in 2008 (n=41) and 2009 (n=39), and the numbers were only slightly lower than were observed in 2007 (n=49). The configuration of this subsite benefited from a landslide in 2006 that provided a larger sandy substrate for adult females to use beginning in 2007 (Figure 6).

15

**Figure 6.** (a) A large landslide occurred at DSB in 2006-7 and (b) created habitat for seals breeding in 2008 and 2009. Photographs by Sarah Allen.

Productivity at DB declined from 2007 to 2009 (0.95, 0.86 and 0.77, respectively; Table 1). This overall decline in productivity reflects a contrasting increase in the adjusted maximum number of adult females between the years (154, 247, and 198, respectively; Table 1). Density dependence mortality of pups may explain in part the decline in productivity since haul out space on DB above the high tide area is limited. During very high tides the beach is awash.

## Environmental Indicators

Elephant seals have an enormous range and migrate one of the longest distances of any mammal (Allen and Mortenson 2011). They forage throughout the North Pacific as far as Alaska rather than seeking prey in the California Current, and so they respond less to regional perturbations in annual upwelling patterns. El Nino Southern Oscillation (ENSO) events, though, may have an effect on elephant seals because elevated sea levels and storm waves wash pups out to sea (Sydeman and Allen 1999). Elephant seals experience a lag effect from such perturbations because of their life history cycle. Elephant seal adult females have been documented to skip a breeding cycle following ENSO events (LeBoeuf and Laws 1992). Such a delayed effect may explain in part the lack of population growth shortly after the 1998 ENSO at PORE. The previous 1992-1993 ENSO might also have affected lower numbers because the lower number of pups produced then would have contributed to a smaller cohort of breeders in 1998-99. The years 2007-2009 were not ENSO years, but indicated a strong La Nina period. Delayed upwelling altered nearshore coastal ocean ecosystems in 2005 (Barth et al. 2007, Peterson et al. 2006) and since then there have been several oceanic anomalies in the North Pacific noted by NOAA (http://www.cpc.noaa.gov/products/CDB/CDB_Archive_html/ accessed July 9, 2010). In the summer of 2007 and into the spring of 2009, there were strong La Nina events with colder than normal sea surface temperatures across large portions of the central and east-central equatorial Pacific, and these anomalies were similar to those following the last strong La Niña episode in 1998-2000 (Figure 7).

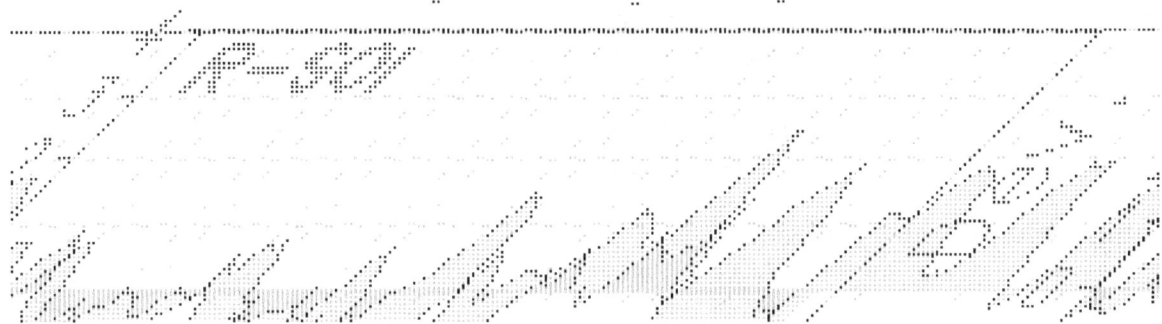

**Figure 7.** Three-month running mean of a CDAS/Reanalysis-derived Southern Oscillation Index (RSOI). Anomalies are departures from the 1979-1995 base period means and are normalized by the mean annual standard deviation (NOAA 2010).

The winters of 2007-08 and 2008-09 were moderate in rainfall but the timing of storms may have caused females to shift from PRH to DB (Figure 8). Locally, storm activities were greater during January in the winter of 2007-08 followed by a milder winter in 2008-09 with more rain falling in February after the peak pupping period. DB continued to be a more attractive sub-colony than PRH during winters with hazardous coastal weather and elevated tide conditions coinciding with the initial arrival of most adult females in January. In contrast, during the milder winter in 2008-09 fewer adult females were displaced to DB from PRH. Mild winter weather may have contributed to lower pup mortality.

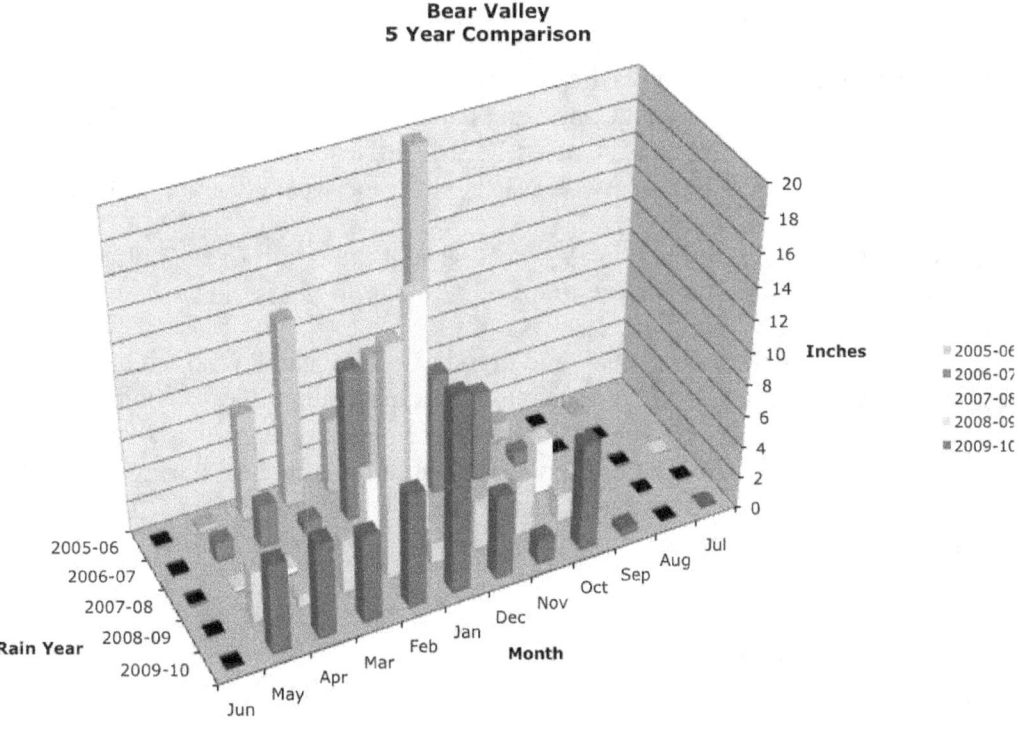

**Figure 8.** A comparison of monthly rainfall at Point Reyes from the winter of 2005-06 to 2009-10. Note large rainfall in January 2007-08 and February 2008-09 (NPS unpublished weather data from Bear Valley Headquarters).

Climate patterns may not only affect annual productivity, but Lee and Sydeman (2009) reported that female seals were more likely to give birth to male pups during ENSO years, indicating that nutritionally stressed pregnant females may be more likely to give birth to male pups than female pups. Such correlations would be difficult to study at PORE because researchers mostly survey seals from a distance, precluding determination of sex.

## Tagging and Tag Resighting

The majority of resight survey visits each year are made at DB, SB and GUS colony sites because of ease of access. We have not calculated the amount of hours of tag resighting effort but usually resighting of tags occurs two days per week with each site visited a minimum of four times per season. A greater proportion of tagging activities and resighting of tags occurred at these sites, and greater effort likely influenced a greater proportion of tagged females recorded at these sites.

Interesting additional tag sightings include:

- The alpha male on DB in 2008 was the 2007 alpha male of Gus' Cove.

- An immature seal tagged at Benitos Islands, Baja, was sighted at DB in 2007-08 and 2008-09.

- A pup born at PORE in 2008 was observed between December 26 and 30, 2008 at Witty's Lagoon on the east coast of Vancouver Island, British Columbia. The yearling was reportedly "alive, in good body condition."

- A female elephant seal that had plastic strapping around the neck in 2007 (which was removed by The Marine Mammal Center and park biologists) was observed in 2008 and 2009 with a pup each year at Gus's Cove. She still had a scar from where the strapping material cut into her neck, but otherwise was healthy and weaned a pup both years.

- A female tagged as a weaned pup in 1995 was seen at the South Beach colony for the second year in a row, successfully raising a pup. She is 14 years old.

- In March 2008, a female born in 1987 and branded at Año Nuevo arrived at DB during the breeding season. She was not pregnant and was one of the oldest females ever recorded at Point Reyes or elsewhere (Figure 9; 21 years old; P. Morris pers. comm.). This female was first observed at PRH in 1989 as an immature seal during the molt and was subsequently observed over many years at PRH with pups. This was the first time, though, that she had been observed at DB.

**Figure 9.** a) Adult female with brand born at Año Nuevo and b) inset of brand. This female was 21 years old and arrived at Drakes Beach at the end of the breeding season, not pregnant. Photographs by Heather Jensen

## Other Research

In early December 2008 and 2009, immature elephant seals with satellite tags applied by scientists at Año Nuevo were seen in the DB colony. In both instances, field staff of Sonoma State University under Dr. Dan Crocker retrieved the tags.

Zeno et al. (2010) analyzed tag resight data combining information collected at PORE with that of several other colonies (Farallon Islands, Año Nuevo, and Piedras Blancas) into a master database. Preliminary analyses indicate that only 16% of females born at PORE disperse to breed at other colonies but that 15% of females born at Piedras Blancas disperse to pup at PORE (Figure 10).

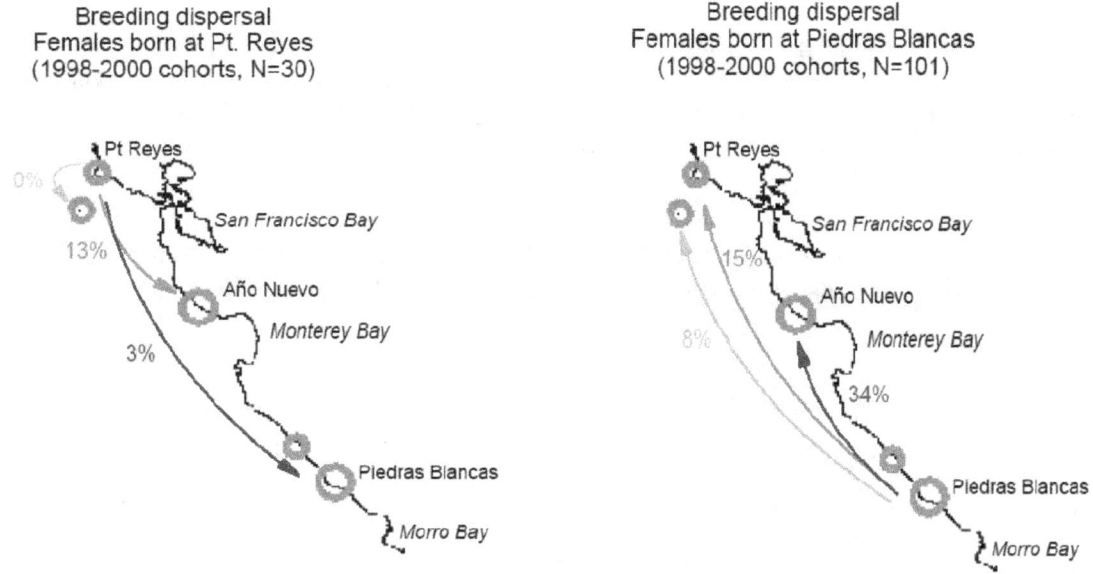

**Figure 10.** Breeding dispersal of females born at (a) PORE and (b) Piedras Blancas (Zeno et al. 2010).

## Operational Issues

### Safety

There were no safety accidents over the two seasons covered by this report. The NPS Job Hazard Analysis (Adams et al. 2009) requires partnering during field work, coupled with a strong mentoring program. The program relies on well experienced volunteers and no one applies tags to seals without another person acting as a safety look-out. Before entering onto a beach with seals, field staff discuss field objectives, timing, and a safety plan for that day's beach visit.

Due to the high numbers of seals on the PRH site and increased breeding and fighting activity during January and February, access to the PRH site was limited to December and late February through mid-March. Because of the high level of cliff erosion, visitation of subsites such as DSB, GUS and CRC are limited and access is assessed each season and throughout the season. In addition, in mid-March Common Murres (*Uria aalge*) start attending nesting sites at the Point Reyes Headlands, so we minimize visits to reduce potential disturbance to nesting seabirds in the last two weeks of March.

### Personnel

The same number of personnel has worked on the monitoring program over the past two years. One permanent staff dedicated approximately 10-15% of her time between December and March training field staff, surveying, tagging, dye-marking and resighting. Two Marin Conservation Corps-Americorps program members, an NPS Biological Technician; and a biologist from The Marine Mammal Center conducted field surveys, tagged seals, resighted tags, and managed data. The Marin Conservation Corps-Americorps members trained and coordinated four long-term volunteers, to assist in population surveys. They also were responsible for most of the data entry and data/error checking, and working with the Point Reyes I&M Database Manager.

The elephant seal docent program trained 60-70 people each year prior to the winter season. In 2008 the docents logged 1,923 hours while contacting some 18,993 park visitors that visited the elephant seal colony overlooks. In 2009, 57 docents logged 2,152 hours while contacting some 19,000 park visitors.

### Permits

In 2007, NMFS reissued a research permit to PRBO Conservation Science which includes Point Reyes National Seashore research. The permit number is 373-1868-00 and is effective until 2012.

# Literature Cited

Adams, D., H. Jensen, H. Nevins, K. Truchinski, D. Roberts, and S. Allen. 2008. Northern elephant seal monitoring 2005-2007 report, Point Reyes National Seashore. Natural Resource Technical Report NPS/SFAN/NRTR—2008/085. National Park Service, Fort Collins, Colorado.

Adams, D., D. Press, M. Hester, H. Nevins, D. Roberts, B. Becker, H. Jensen, E. Flynn, M. Koenen, and S. Allen. 2009. San Francisco Bay Area Network pinniped monitoring protocol. Natural Resource Report NPS/SFAN/NRR—2009/170. National Park Service, Fort Collins, Colorado.

Adams, J. 1994. Status of the Northern elephant seal, *Mirounga angustirostris* (Gill, 1866), breeding at Point Reyes Headlands, California during 1992-1993. Senior thesis. University of California, Santa Cruz, California. 29 pp.

Allen, S. G. 1995. Northern elephant seal management plan for Point Reyes National Seashore. Report to the National Park Service. 35 pp.

Allen, S. G., S. C. Peaslee, and H. R. Huber. 1989. Colonization by northern elephant seals of the Point Reyes Peninsula, California. Marine Mammal Science 5(3):298-302.

Allen, S., and J. Mortenson. 2011. Field guide to marine mammals of the Pacific Coast: Baja, California, Oregon, Washington, British Columbia. University of California Press, Berkeley, California.

Barlow, J., P. Boveng, M. S. Lowry, B. S. Stewart, B. J. Le Boeuf, W. J. Sydeman, R. J. Jameson, S. G. Allen, and C.W. Oliver. 1993. Status of the northern elephant seal population along the U.S. West Coast in 1992. Administrative Report LJ-93-01. Southwest Fisheries Science Center, National Marine Fisheries Service, La Jolla, California. 32 pp.

Barth, J. A., B. A. Menge, J. Lubchenco, F. Chan, J. M. Bane, A. R. Kirincich, M. A. McManus, K .J. Nielsen, S. D. Pierce, and L. Washburn. 2007. Delayed upwelling alters nearshore coastal ocean ecosystems in the northern California current. Proceedings of the National Academy of Sciences. 104(10):3719-3724.

Boveng, P. 1988. Status of the northern elephant seal population on the U.S. West Coast. Administrative Report LJ-88-05. Southwest Fisheries Science Center, National Marine Fisheries Service, La Jolla, California. 35pp.

Condit, R., B. J. Le Boeuf, P.A. Morris, and M. Sylvan. 2007. Estimating population size in asynchronous aggregations: a Bayesian approach and test with elephant seal censuses. Marine Mammal Science 23(4):834-855.

LeBoeuf, B. J., and R. M. Laws 1992. Elephant seals. University of California Press, Berkeley, California. 414 pp.

Lee, D. 2006. Population size and reproductive success of northern elephant seals on the South Farallon Islands 2005-2006. Report to U. S. Fish and Wildlife Service, Farallon National Wildlife Refuge, San Francisco, California. 9 pp.

Lee, D. E., and W. J. Sydeman. 2009. North Pacific climate mediates offspring sex ratio in northern elephant seals. Journal of Mammalogy 90:1–8.

McCann, T. S. 1985. Size, status and demography of southern elephant seal (*Mirounga leonina*) populations. Pages 1-17 *in* J. K. Ling and M. M. Bryden, editors. Studies of sea mammals in south latitudes. South Australian Museum, Adelaide, Australia. 132 pp.

National Oceanic and Atmospheric Administration (NOAA). 2010. Climate of 2010 El Niño/Southern Oscillation (ENSO). Available from http://www.cpc.noaa.gov/products/CDB/CDB_Archive_html/ (accessed 9 July 2010).

Peterson, W. T., R. Emmett, R. Goericke, E. Venrick, A. Mantyla, S. J. Bograd, F. B. Schwing, R. Hewitt, N. Lo, W. Watson, and others. 2006. The state of the California current, 2005-2006: Warm in the north, cool in the south. CalCOFI Report 47:30-74.

Pettee, J. 1999. Factors affecting distribution and reproductive success in elephant seals (*Mirounga angustirostris*) at Point Reyes. Thesis. San Francisco State University, San Francisco, California.

Stewart, B. S., P. K. Yochem, H. R. Huber, R. L. DeLong, R. J. Jameson, W. J. Sydeman, S. G. Allen, and B. J. LeBoeuf. 1994. History and present status of the northern elephant seal population. Pages 29-48 *in* B. J. Le Boeuf and R. M. Laws, editors. Elephant seals: population ecology, behavior, and physiology. University of California Press, Berkeley, California.

Sydeman, W. J., and S. G. Allen. 1999. Pinniped population dynamics in central California: correlations with sea surface temperature and upwelling indices. Marine Mammal Science 15:446-461.

Zeno, R., R. Condit, B. Hatfield, D. Lee, S. G. Allen. 2010. Population trends for the Point Reyes National Seashore northern elephant seal colony and predictions for future growth. Poster at Natural Resources and Science Conference for the San Francisco Bay Area Network of National Parks, February 4, 2010.

# Appendix A

**Table App A.1.** Elephant seal flipper tags seen at Point Reyes National Seashore from other sites during the 2007-2008 breeding season.

| Date | Subsite | Maturity | Sex | Left Tag Color[1] | Left Tag #[2] | Right Tag Color[1] | Right Tag #[2] | Pup Size |
|------|---------|----------|-----|------------|-----------|-------------|------------|----------|
| 24-Dec-07 | LTH | YRLNG | U | GR | U952 | | NT | |
| 02-Jan-08 | NDB | ADULT | F | WH | X116 | | NT | |
| 14-Jan-08 | NDB | YRLNG | U | GR | U806 | | NS | |
| 14-Jan-08 | NDB | ADULT | F | | NS | RE | 4361 | |
| 17-Jan-08 | NDB | ADULT | F | WH | X116 | | NS | P1 |
| 17-Jan-08 | NDB | ADULT | F | | NT | YE | Y721 | |
| 17-Jan-08 | NDB | YRLNG | U | GR | U806 | | NS | |
| 17-Jan-08 | NDB | ADULT | F | | NS | RE | 4361 | P2 |
| 17-Jan-08 | NDB | YRLNG | U | | NS | WH | T877 | |
| 28-Jan-08 | NDB | YRLNG | U | | NS | BLUE | 68 | |
| 28-Jan-08 | NDB | ADULT | F | | NS | YE | Y724 | P3 |
| 28-Jan-08 | NDB | ADULT | F | GR | 7_54 | | NS | P2 |
| 28-Jan-08 | NDB | ADULT | F | WH | X892 | | NS | P1 |
| 28-Jan-08 | NDB | ADULT | F | | NT | RE | 4006 | |
| 28-Jan-08 | NDB | ADULT | F | GR | NR | PK | NR | P3 |
| 28-Jan-08 | NDB | ADULT | F | | NS | WH | 251 | P2 |
| 01-Feb-08 | LTH | SA3 | M | WH | X888 | | NT | |
| 07-Feb-08 | GUS | ADULT | F | PU | 859 | | NS | P3 |
| 07-Feb-08 | GUS | ADULT | F | | NT | WH | X668 | P3 |
| 07-Feb-08 | GUS | ADULT | F | | NS | OR | 6537 | P3 |
| 07-Feb-08 | NDB | ADULT | F | GR | BT | | | P3 |
| 07-Feb-08 | NDB | ADULT | F | GR | R877 | PK | NR | P2 |
| 07-Feb-08 | NDB | ADULT | F | WH | X892 | | NT | P2 |
| 07-Feb-08 | NDB | ADULT | F | | NS | RE | 4006 | |
| 07-Feb-08 | NDB | ADULT | F | | NS | GR | K954 | P3 |
| 07-Feb-08 | NDB | ADULT | F | WH | X54 | PK | NR | P3 |
| 11-Feb-08 | DSB | ADULT | F | | NT | YE | X874 | P3 |
| 15-Feb-08 | NDB | ADULT | F | | | WH | X852 | P2 |
| 15-Feb-08 | NDB | ADULT | F | WH | X54 | PK | J165 | P3 |
| 15-Feb-08 | NDB | ADULT | F | | | RE | 4006 | P3 |

[1] Año Nuevo (GR) Piedras Blancas (WH) San Nicholas Island (RE), San Miguel/Santa Rosa Islands (YE), Southeast Farallon Islands (PK with different letters),  Marine Mammal Center (OR).

[2] An underscore in the tag number refers to an unread digit; no tag present (NT), no tag seen (NS), tag seen but not read (NR).

**Table App A.1.** Elephant seal flipper tags seen at Point Reyes National Seashore from other sites during the 2007-2008 breeding season (continued).

| Date | Subsite | Maturity | Sex | Left Tag Color[1] | Left Tag #[2] | Right Tag Color[1] | Right Tag #[2] | Pup Size |
|------|---------|----------|-----|-------------------|---------------|--------------------|----------------|----------|
| 15-Feb-08 | NDB | ADULT | F | | | GR | 0967 | P2 |
| 20-Feb-08 | NDB | ADULT | F | WH | X892 | | NS | P4 |
| 25-Feb-08 | NDB | ADULT | F | | NS | WH | X251 | P3 |
| 28-Feb-08 | NUN | SA3 | M | | NT | OR | 43701 | |
| 28-Feb-08 | NUN | SA3 | M | WH | X642 | | NT | |
| 28-Feb-08 | NUN | SA3 | M | GR | NR | GR | NR | |
| 03-Mar-08 | C1 | ADULT | F | GR | 3452 | | NS | |
| 03-Mar-08 | C2 | SA2 | M | | NT | WH | T314 | |
| 03-Mar-08 | C2 | ADULT | F | | NS | GR | 1241 | P3 |
| 04-Mar-08 | GUS | ADULT | F | WH | T018 | | NS | P3 |
| 06-Mar-08 | DSB | SA2 | M | | NT | WH | T014 | |

[1]Año Nuevo (GR) Piedras Blancas (WH) San Nicholas Island (RE), San Miguel/Santa Rosa Islands (YE), Southeast Farallon Islands (PK with different letters),  Marine Mammal Center (OR).

[2] An underscore in the tag number refers to an unread digit; no tag present (NT), no tag seen (NS), tag seen but not read (NR).

**Table App A.2.** Elephant seal flipper tags seen at Point Reyes National Seashore from other sites during the 2008-2009 breeding season.

| Date | Subsite | Maturity | Sex | Left Tag Color[1] | Left Tag #[2] | Right Tag color[1] | Right Tag #[2] | Pup Size |
|------|---------|----------|-----|-------------------|---------------|--------------------|----------------|----------|
| 12-Nov-08 | NDB | IMM | U | | NT | GR | X350 | |
| 12-Nov-08 | NDB | IMM | U | WH | V705 | | NT | |
| 12-Nov-08 | NDB | YRLNG | U | | NT | GR | X118 | |
| 12-Nov-08 | NDB | IMM | F | | NT | YE | 1733 | |
| 12-Nov-08 | NDB | IMM | F | WH | V782 | | NT | |
| 12-Nov-08 | NDB | IMM | M | WH | V791 | | NT | |
| 12-Nov-08 | NDB | IMM | U | WH | V563 | | NT | |
| 10-Dec-08 | NDB | YRLNG | | GR | U52 | GR | X300 | |
| 10-Dec-08 | NDB | IMM | | | | GR | U791 | |
| 10-Dec-08 | NDB | SA3 | M | | | WH | T174 | |
| 11-Dec-08 | NDB | YRLNG | F | GR | U52 | | | |
| 11-Dec-08 | NDB | SA3 | M | | | WH | T174 | |
| 16-Jan-09 | GUS | ADULT | F | WH | T01_ | | | P1 |
| 16-Jan-09 | GUS | ADULT | F | WH | __66 | WH | NR | |
| 16-Jan-09 | NDB | ADULT | F | | NT | OR | 6505 | |
| 22-Jan-09 | GUS | ADULT | F | | NT | WH | _668 | P2 |
| 22-Jan-09 | GUS | ADULT | F | | NT | WH | 668 | P2 |
| 22-Jan-09 | NDB | IMM | F | GR | __77 | | NA | |
| 22-Jan-09 | NDB | UNKN | F | GR | __77 | | NS | |
| 22-Jan-09 | NDB | ADULT | F | | | YE | Y__ | P2 |
| 22-Jan-09 | NDB | ADULT | F | | NS | WH | X307 | |
| 22-Jan-09 | NDB | ADULT | F | | | YE | X5__ | |
| 28-Jan-09 | NDB | ADULT | F | | NS | YE | Y125 | P2 |
| 28-Jan-09 | NDB | ADULT | F | WH | X892 | | NS | |
| 28-Jan-09 | NDB | SA3 | M | | NS | WH | NR | |
| 30-Jan-09 | LTH | ADULT | F | | | GR | L227 | P1 |
| 30-Jan-09 | LTH | SA4 | M | | | GR | NR | |
| 30-Jan-09 | LTH | SA3 | M | | NT | WH | T087 | |
| 30-Jan-09 | NDB | UNKN | F | GR | 3877 | | NS | |
| 02-Feb-09 | NDB | ADULT | F | WH | 1322 | | NS | P4 |

[1]Año Nuevo (GR) Piedras Blancas (WH) San Nicholas Island (RE), San Miguel/Santa Rosa Islands (YE), Southeast Farallon Islands (PK with different letters), Marine Mammal Center (OR.

[2] An underscore in the tag number refers to an unread digit; no tag present (NT), no tag seen (NS), tag seen but not read (NR).

**Table App A.2.** Elephant seal flipper tags seen at Point Reyes National Seashore from other sites during the 2008-2009 breeding season (continued).

| Date | Subsite | Maturity | Sex | Left Tag Color[1] | Left Tag #[2] | Right Tag color[1] | Right Tag #[2] | Pup Size |
|---|---|---|---|---|---|---|---|---|
| 02-Feb-09 | NDB | ADULT | F | GR | | | | P3 |
| 02-Feb-09 | NDB | ADULT | F | | NS | WH | X897 | P1 |
| 06-Feb-09 | NDB | ADULT | F | WH | X892 | | NS | P2 |
| 06-Feb-09 | NDB | ADULT | F | | NS | YE | Y72_ | P4 |
| 06-Feb-09 | NDB | ADULT | F | GR | 0235 | | NS | P3 |
| 06-Feb-09 | NDB | ADULT | F | PU | 869 | | NT | P3 |
| 12-Feb-09 | NDB | ADULT | F | WH | X892 | | NS | P2 |
| 18-Feb-09 | DSB | ADULT | F | GR | NR | | NT | P2 |
| 20-Feb-09 | NDB | SA4 | M | WH | T174 | | | |
| 05-Mar-09 | LTH | SA4 | M | OR | NR | | | |
| 06-Mar-09 | NDB | SA2 | M | | NT | GR | T396 | |
| 18-Mar-09 | C1 | ADULT | F | | NT | WH | 0258 | |
| 18-Mar-09 | TIP | SA2 | M | | | WH | T467 | |
| 18-Mar-09 | TIP | ADULT | F | | | WH | _98 | |
| 18-Mar-09 | TIP | IMM | U | | | WH | V785 | |
| 19-Mar-09 | TIP | SA3 | M | GR | 2658 | | NT | |
| 19-Mar-09 | TIP | IMM | U | WH | V271 | | NT | |

[1]Año Nuevo (GR) Piedras Blancas (WH) San Nicholas Island (RE), San Miguel/Santa Rosa Islands (YE), Southeast Farallon Islands (PK with different letters), Marine Mammal Center (OR).

[2] An underscore in the tag number refers to an unread digit; no tag present (NT), no tag seen (NS), tag seen but not read (NR).

NPS 612/118228, December 2012